THE GREAT ST. JOSEPH

Dr. Remi Amelunxen

Copyright © 2008 by Remi Amelunxen

All rights reserved. No part of this book may be reproduced or transmitted in any form or by any means whatsoever, including the Internet, without permission in writing from the author, except that brief selections may be quoted or copied for non-profit use without permission, provided full credit is given.

ISBN: 978-0-9726516-9-1
Library of Congress Number: 2008932450

Printed and bound in the United States

Cover: TIA's art desk.

Tradition in Action, Inc.
P.O. Box 23135
Los Angeles, CA 90023
www.TraditionInAction.org

I dedicate this book to my dear aunt,
Clare Rita DenHaerynck,
with heartfelt appreciation for her assistance and support
in bringing this manuscript on St. Joseph to print.

My sincere gratitude also to Dr. Marian T. Horvat
and Mr. Atila S. Guimarães for their work in
reviewing and editing this book.

It is indeed a pleasure for me to be a part of the
work-team of Tradition in Action.

R.A.

Table of Contents

Prayer 9

Introduction 11

Chap. 1: Sanctification in the Womb 17

Chap. 2: Presentation of St. Joseph in the Temple 21

Chap. 3: Joseph's Childhood 23

Chap. 4: Departure from Nazareth to Jerusalem 25

Chap. 5: Espousal of St. Joseph with the Blessed Virgin Mary 27

Chap. 6: St. Joseph and the Blessed Mother before the Incarnation 31

Chap. 7: The Incarnation of Our Lord Jesus Christ, and the Visitation of Holy Mary with St. Elizabeth 35

Chap. 8: How St. Joseph Was Informed of the Incarnation ... 39

Chap. 9: The Nativity of Our Lord Jesus Christ 43

Chap. 10: The Circumcision of the Infant Jesus and His Presentation in the Temple 53

Chap. 11: The Flight into Egypt, the Massacre of the Holy Innocents, and the Return to Nazareth 63

Chap. 12: St. Joseph's Life at Nazareth and the Finding of the Child Jesus in the Temple 69

Chap. 13: The Suffering and Death of St. Joseph and Evidence of His Assumption into Heaven 75

Appendix 1: Quotes in Holy Scripture regarding St. Joseph ... 85

Appendix 2: The Holy Family Belonged to a Royal House 89

Appendix 3: Clarifications 93

Prayer

The following prayer to St. Joseph was found in the fiftieth year of Our Lord and Savior Jesus Christ. In 1505 Pope Julian II sent it to Emperor Charles V of the Holy Roman Empire when he was going into battle. Sacred Tradition says that whoever reads this prayer, hears it, or carries it will never die a sudden death, nor be drowned, nor shall poison take an effect on him, nor shall he be burned in any fire. It is as follows:

O St. Joseph, whose protection is so great, so strong, so powerful before the throne of God, I place in thee all my interests and desires. O St. Joseph, do assist me by thy powerful intercession and obtain for me from thy Divine Son all spiritual blessings, through Jesus Christ Our Lord, so that having engaged here below thy heavenly power, I may offer my thanksgiving and homage to the most loving of Fathers.

O St. Joseph, I never weary contemplating thee and Jesus asleep in thy arms. I dare not approach while He reposes near thy heart. Press Him in my name and kiss His fine head for me and ask Him to return the kiss when I draw my dying breath. St. Joseph, Patron of departing souls, pray for me. Amen.

Imprimatur by Bishop George Ahr of Trenton, New Jersey.

A very powerful daily prayer!

March 19 is celebrated as the feast day of St. Joseph

Introduction

A large part of the present account of the life of St. Joseph was taken from a massive and very old work entitled *Life of the Blessed Virgin* by Msgr. Romuald Gentilucci, Chamberlain of Honor to His Holiness Pope Pius IX, now Blessed, dated 1856. The full title is *Life of the Blessed Virgin, of Her Blessed Spouse, St. Joseph, and Her Holy Parents St. Joachim and St. Anne.* At the beginning of the work is a beautiful letter of Msgr. Gentilucci dedicating the text to His Holiness Pope Pius IX . In one passage, the Monsignor stated:

"I was sustained and encouraged by the incalculable protection which the Sovereign Pontiff Pius IX deigned to bestow on my work, even permitting it to be adorned with his august name. The words of veneration and love for the Virgin Mary which he uttered on that occasion determined me to overcome every obstacle and bear this humble offering to Mary's altar."

It should be remembered that Pope Pius IX declared the dogma of the Immaculate Conception on December 8, 1854, four years prior to its declaration by the Blessed Mother to Bernadette Soubirous at Lourdes in France in 1858.

The present work is based principally on Part Two of Msgr. Gentilucci's compilation, which brings together his own and two other studies on St. Joseph. Part Two is authored by Fr. Joseph Ignatius Vallejo, S.J., and its extended title is *The Life of St. Joseph, Spouse of the Blessed Virgin Mary and Foster Father of Jesus*. Fr. Vallejo was born in Mexico in 1718 and was a Professor of Theology at the University of St. Francis Borgia in Guatemala. Pope Pius IX approved this discourse by Fr. Vallejo and based on it, proclaimed St. Joseph as Patron of the Universal Church. He is also recognized as the patron saint of the family, the worker and the New World (the three Americas).

Fr. Vallejo's discourse is a lengthy 342 pages on the life of St. Joseph. Since his writings are quite detailed, our goal was to select important events in his life and present them in simpler form.

Other significant episodes from the life of St. Joseph, containing related events in the lives of the Blessed Mother and Jesus and not included in the work by Fr. Vallejo, were taken from *The Mystical City of God* by Ven. Mary of Agreda, which is an extensive four-volume account of the lives of the Holy Family.

The following is a brief history of the life of this remarkable mystic. Mary of Agreda was born on

April 2, 1602 in the small town of Agreda near Tarazona in Spain. In 1617, she entered the Convent of the Immaculate Conception in Agreda, home of the Discalced Franciscan Nuns. In 1625, she became Abbess, and her fame spread in both the Church and the State. King Philip IV visited her several times to consult on State affairs. Ven. Mary of Agreda is known to have been favored with the miraculous gift of bilocation.[1] Always remaining in her convent in Agreda, she was for a number of years the first messenger of the Holy Faith sent by God to the Indians in Arizona and New Mexico. This occurred prior to the missionary activity of the Franciscans, who were amazed at the testimony of the Indians about the beautiful lady who instructed them in the Catholic Faith.

According to Ven. Mary of Agreda, by divine command she began to write *The Mystical City of God* on December 8, 1655, the feast of the Immaculate Conception. One year after her death in 1665, she was declared Venerable and the process of canonization was promoted. In 1681 Pope Innocent XI decreed that *The Mystical City of God* be freely spread among the clergy and laity. Why this great mystic has not yet been canonized remains a mystery.

---

1. This is revealed in *The Mystical City of God*, Vol. I, *The Conception*, on the page opposite "Contents."

The events in the life of St. Joseph found in the short Chapters 2, 3 and 4 were taken from *The Life of St. Joseph as Manifested by Our Lord Jesus Christ to Maria Cecilia Baij, O.S.B.,* Abbess of the Benedictine Convent of St. Peter in Montefiascone, Italy from 1743-1766. This work of Abbess Baij has the *nihil obstat* and *imprimatur* of Bishop Emidio Trenta Bishop of Viterbo, Italy, 1921. It also has the approval of Pope Benedict XV and learned theologians.

Some of the notables referenced by Fr. Vallejo include: St. Ambrose, St. Justin, St. Basil, St. Leo, St. Jerome, St. John Chrysostom, St. Bernard, St. Augustine, St. Thomas Aquinas, St. Peter Canisius, St. Remigius, St. Teresa of Avila, St. Alphonsus Liguori, St. Francis de Sales, St. Bernardine of Sienna, and Fr. Bernardine de Busto, a confrere of St. Bernardine of Sienna. Also referenced many times are Fr. Francisco Suarez, a great theologian of the 16th century; Fr. Segneri, a reputed theologian of the 17th century, and Abbot Trombelli, also a noted theologian. In addition, more than a dozen eminent lay historians and lay theologians are also listed in this work.

Since Sacred Scripture is sparse on the details of the life of St. Joseph,[2] to obtain insight into the

---

2. See Appendix 1.

great marvels of his life and that of the Holy Family, we must rely on other sources such as Sacred Tradition, the writings of the Doctors of the Church, Saints, eminent lay historians and theologians, and the writings and revelations of approved mystics. Msgr. Gentilucci's three-part book incorporates these sources, except for the works of approved mystics.

It must be emphasized that all of the sources used are not *de fide* and belief by the faithful is not mandatory regarding them. However, it should be stressed that these works have received the approbation of Popes, Doctors of the Church, and many Saints, which lends great credibility to their authenticity. For example, *The Mystical City of God* by Ven. Mary of Agreda has received the approbation of 32 Popes, and the great St. Pius X so loved the work that he recommended daily reading from it for the clergy and laity.

* * *

Chapter 1

SANCTIFICATION IN THE WOMB

God permitted the marriage of St. Joseph's parents Jacob and Rachel to be unfruitful for a period of time even though both led very holy lives. After much prayer, fasting, almsgiving and pilgrimages, God answered their prayer for the desired offspring chosen by Heaven for them.

While praying in the Temple, Joseph's mother Rachel was inspired to know that she would conceive. At this time, three unusually brilliant stars appeared shining directly above their domicile, which were seen only by Jacob and Rachel. The three stars are interpreted to mean that Joseph was destined to establish the terrestrial Trinity and become the head of the Holy Family.

As the time of Joseph's birth approached, Rachel prepared with continual prayer. The birth took place with great ease, and the tiny babe had a most angelic expression. The holy child Joseph was born most beautiful and perfect of body. The three stars again appeared over the abode where Joseph was born. This time they were observed by many occupants of Nazareth who in astonishment wondered at their meaning.

As written by St. Bernard, the Triune God destined that St. Joseph possess the most honorable position ever witnessed by the Angels and the Saints.[3] Heaven thus prepared St. Joseph to be the Spouse of the Blessed Virgin Mary and the foster Father of Jesus and, as such, he acted as the alter God the Father on earth. He was thus endowed with virtues and privileges above all men.

It is stated in Sacred Scripture (Matt 11:7-19) that St. John the Baptist was the holiest of men born of woman. The eminent theologian of the 16th century Fr. Francisco Suarez states, however, that this did not include the Hypostatic Order (the Holy Family) of which St. Joseph was the head, and that St. Joseph is indeed the holiest of all men born of woman. He is thus superior to St. John the Baptist and the Apostles. While St. Thomas Aquinas and other Doctors of the Church place St. John the Baptist and the Apostles at the head of all the Saints, they also state that St. Joseph is an exception to the clause in Sacred Scripture.[4]

Fr. Paolo Segneri, S.J. (1624), an esteemed theologian, speaks eloquently of St. Joseph: "Joseph

---

3. Fr. Joseph Ignatius Vallejo, S.J., *The Life of St. Joseph, Spouse of the Blessed Virgin Mary and Foster Father of Jesus* (New York: Thomas Kelly, 1856), p. 13.

4. *Ibid.*, p. 29.

was ennobled and singularly privileged with the honor of being spouse of the Mother of God: a dignity which is a solid principle from which it follows with every mark of probability that St. Joseph was not only sanctified in his mother's womb, but that he was afterwards confirmed in grace and exempt from all evil so that no man – we can boldly say no man on this earth ever was holier than Joseph." [5]

Joseph was of the tribe of Judah, of the noble blood of the House of David. He was the first born of Jacob of Nazareth and Rachel of Bethlehem. In his work, Fr. Vallejo confirms and gives more details about the marvelous preparation of Providence for St. Joseph. He specifies that Joseph was sanctified in the womb of his mother seven months after his conception, and that original sin was removed and all sin destroyed in him for the entire course of his life, as happened with the Precursor.[6] Indeed, as taught by Sacred Tradition, St. John the Baptist was sanctified in the womb of St. Elizabeth. Ven. Mary of Agreda comments that Holy Mary hastened to visit her cousin Elizabeth to procure without delay the sanctification of the Precursor of the Incarnate Word.[7]

---

5. *Ibid.*, p. 24.

6. *Ibid.*

7. Ven. Mary of Agreda, *The Mystical City of God,* Vol. II, *The Incarnation,* p. 162.

While the Blessed Mother had the entire use of reason from birth, St. Joseph received partial use of reason soon after his birth, and then full use in his third year, when he was endowed with infused knowledge and his soul augmented with new graces and virtues.[8]

St. John Chrysostom writes that St. Joseph and the Blessed Mother were born in Bethlehem.[9]

* * *

---

8. *Ibid.,* Vol. III, *The Transfixion,* p. 164.
9. Fr. Vallejo, *The Life of St. Joseph,* p. 43.

Chapter 2

PRESENTATION OF ST. JOSEPH IN THE TEMPLE [10]

Jacob and Rachel set out for Jerusalem 40 days after the birth of the child as prescribed by the Jewish law. Rachel went to the Temple for the rite of her purification and to present and offer Joseph to God. An Angel spoke to Jacob and Rachel in dreams disclosing that the child would have the singular privilege of living with the promised Messiah. They were told not to divulge this secret to Joseph.

During Rachel's rite of purification and the presentation of Joseph, she received heavenly insights into the gifts of Joseph and how divine grace was diffused into his soul. As the Priest returned Joseph to his mother, God revealed to him that Joseph was chosen for an exalted mission. Little Joseph was totally immersed in love of God after his presentation even though he had not yet attained the full use of reason.

In addition to his regular Guardian Angel, Joseph had another Angel assigned to him by God who would speak to him often in dreams and who would

---

10. Abbess Maria Cecilia Baij, O.S.B, *The Life of St. Joseph,* (Asbury, NJ: 101 Foundation, 1997), pp. 6-7.

instruct him in all that was required of him, making him even more pleasing in the eyes of God. Joseph's first words were "My God," taught to him by the Angel.

* * *

Chapter 3

Joseph's Childhood [11]

After attaining the full use of reason, Joseph advanced to the reading of the Sacred Scripture, which Jacob explained to him. All of his available time was consumed by prayer, reading and reflection. The saintly child was often absorbed by God for days in contemplation and was continuously nourished by divine consolation.

When Joseph was seven-years-old, his special Angel spoke to him, telling him that God had decreed that he was to receive a great and sublime favor. Joseph was receptive to the message, but did not attempt to discover the nature of this signal grace. Even at age seven, Joseph had unusual intellectual capacity. All of his actions had a mature perfection, and his father and mother always consulted Joseph on religious and other important matters. Joseph, being enlightened by God, was never mistaken.

One night as Joseph was sleeping, his special Angel appeared and told him that God was pleased about his resolution to lead a life of perpetual virginity. The Angel presented him a cincture from God as

---

11. *Ibid.*, pp. 7-11.

a sign of approval, and then girded him with the heavenly cincture. The sublime gift Joseph was to receive, that is, to be the Spouse of the Mother of the Incarnate Word, was not revealed to him. His ardent wish and prayer was the privilege of seeing the Messiah.

The Devil, enemy of all that is good, was enraged by the marvelous virtue of Joseph and launched fierce attacks against him from an early age and throughout his life. Joseph withstood all these attacks and never succumbed to the temptations of the Evil One. As he grew older, Joseph made great strides in the practice of virtue, in the love of God, and in the study of Scriptures. He never caused God any displeasure, since his whole life was free of any sin.

* * *

Chapter 4

DEPARTURE FROM NAZARETH TO JERUSALEM [12]

Inspired by his special Angel, at age 20 Joseph left his home in Nazareth and made the journey to Jerusalem. Upon his arrival in Jerusalem, Joseph went immediately to the Temple and renewed his offering to God, begging Him to manifest His holy will. Joseph was directed to seek a carpenter who could teach him the trade he needed to support himself. He soon met a God-fearing man who was a skilled carpenter. After he completed his apprenticeship, he worked a number of years with the master-workman until this good man became seriously ill. Joseph assisted him to obtain a happy death, and then continued the trade on his own.

Joseph lived a life of poverty and penance, and did all with great joy as God filled him with heavenly consolation. Engaged in service in the Temple at this time was the Holy Virgin Mary. Her exceptional virtues made her a source of esteem to all who knew her. Joseph was told by his special Angel about Holy Mary, which filled him with great joy. Joseph knew something awaited him involving Mary, but was not

---

12. *Ibid.*, pp. 47-51.

aware of the great role he was to play in the coming of the Messiah, which both Mary and Joseph so greatly desired.

* * *

Chapter 5

Espousal of St. Joseph with the Blessed Virgin Mary

After the Blessed Virgin Mary reached the age when, according to Hebrew law, she was to leave the Temple, the priests met to decide her state of life since her father Joachim had died. It was concurred that she should marry one of the same tribe and family as her own, the tribe of Judah. The Blessed Mother Mary was at this time thirteen and a half years old. Having made a vow of perpetual virginity, resolving not to have a husband, this decision that she should enter into matrimony caused her much anxiety. Nevertheless, she suspended her judgment and submitted to the will of God.

On the day when the Blessed Mother reached her fourteenth year, the single men who were descendants of the tribe of Judah and the race of David gathered in the Temple in Jerusalem. Among them was St. Joseph who was then 30 years of age. Like Holy Mary, Joseph also had taken a perpetual vow of chastity.

God spoke to the heart of the High Priest, inspiring him to place into the hands of each of the potential spouses a wooden staff. Each prayed to have Mary as spouse. Joseph considered himself unworthy for this honor, resolving anew his vow of chastity. At the same time, he resigned himself to God's will.

While all were in prayer, the staff Joseph held was seen to blossom. Simultaneously, a dove of the purest white and resplendent with brilliant light descended and rested upon the head of St. Joseph. In the interior of his heart God spoke: "Joseph, My servant, Mary shall be thy spouse: Accept her with attentive reverence, for she is agreeable in My eyes, just and most pure in soul and body, and thou shall do all that she shall say to thee." [13]

After this miraculous manifestation of the blossoming of the staff and the presence of the Holy Ghost in the form of a dove, the Priests declared St. Joseph to be the spouse of Mary, chosen by God. St. Joseph was 30 years of age at his espousal to Holy Mary. It is related that the nuptial ring that Joseph gave to the Blessed Virgin is preserved in Perugia, a city of Umbria, Italy, belonging to the dominions of the Church.

Notwithstanding the consecration of her virginity, the Blessed Virgin Mary accepted the union with Joseph. She was given to know by the grace of

---

13. *The Mystical City of God,* Vol. I, *The Conception,* p. 577.

God that both had taken vows of chastity, which would be perpetual. That Mary and Joseph contracted their alliance on the condition of observing perpetual chastity is a Tradition of the Church taught by great theologians over the years.

The motives that God had in choosing St. Joseph as spouse of the Blessed Mother are not written in the Holy Gospels. What we know is from the Sacred Tradition of the Church and the teachings of the Fathers. St. Leo the Great says that God in his decrees consults not only His Divine Omnipotence but also His Infinite Wisdom, and that St. Joseph was chosen to be Holy Mary's spouse because he was of all men the only one perfectly suited to the lofty designs of the Lord.[14]

St. John Chrysostom and St. Bernard affirm that from the time of her espousal to Joseph until the time of the nuptials, Mary was under the guardianship of Joseph. [15]

Having arrived at their home in Nazareth (the Holy House that was transported by the Angels to Loreto, Italy in 1294) where Mary had inherited the possessions and estates of her parents St. Anne and St. Joachim, they were welcomed by their friends

---

14. Fr. Vallejo, *The Life of St. Joseph*, p. 63
15. *Ibid.*, p. 64.

and relatives with the joyful congratulations customary on such occasions.

* * *

Chapter 6

ST. JOSEPH AND THE BLESSED MOTHER
BEFORE THE INCARNATION

During the early time when the Holy Couple were residing in the Holy House in Nazareth, St. Joseph said to his spouse Mary:

"My Spouse and Lady, I give thanks to the Lord Most High God for the favor of having designed me as your husband without my merit, though I judged myself unworthy even of thy company. But His Majesty, Who can raise up the lowly whenever He wishes, showed this mercy to me and I desire and hope, relying on thy discretion and virtue, that thou will help me to make a proper return in serving Him with an upright heart.

"Hold me, therefore, as thy servant and by the true love which I have for thee, I beg thee to supply for my deficiencies in the fulfillment of the domestic duties and of other things which as a worthy husband I should know how to perform. Tell me, my Lady, what is thy pleasure in order that I may fulfill it." [16]

---

16. *The Mystical City of God*, Vol. I, *The Conception*, p. 579.

In the presence of the Blessed Virgin's visible choir of Angels, she responded to St. Joseph:

"My Lord and Spouse, it is just that we give praise and glory with all reverence to Our God and Creator, Who is infinite in goodness and incomprehensible in His judgments. I acknowledge myself among all creatures as more beholden and indebted to Him than all others; for meriting less, I have received from His hands more than they.

"At a tender age, being compelled thereto by the force of the truth which with the knowledge of the deceitfulness of visible things His divine light made known to me, I consecrated myself to God by a perpetual vow of chastity in body and soul. His I am and Him I acknowledge as my Spouse and Lord with fixed resolve to preserve for Him my chastity. I beseech thee, my master, to help me in fulfilling this vow, while in other things I will be thy servant, willing to work for the comfort of thy life as long as mine shall last. Yield, my Spouse, to this resolve and make a like resolve, so we might offer ourselves as an acceptable sacrifice to the eternal God. Then may He receive us in the odor of sweetness and bestow on us the eternal rewards for which we hope." [17]

---

17. *Ibid,* p. 580.

St. Joseph responded:

"I desire thee to know, Lady, that at the age of twelve years, I also made a promise to serve the Most High in perpetual chastity. On that account I now gladly ratify this vow in order not to impede thy own. In the presence of His Majesty, I promise to aid thee in serving Him and loving Him according to thy full desires."[18]

After this marvelous exchange, by divine inspiration the two most holy and chaste spouses felt an incomparable joy and consolation.

* * *

---

18. *Ibid.*, p. 581.

Chapter 7

THE INCARNATION OF OUR LORD JESUS CHRIST, AND THE VISITATION OF HOLY MARY WITH ST. ELIZABETH

A few months after the Holy Couple had resided in Nazareth, the Divine Word was conceived in the womb of the Blessed Mother. The Archangel Gabriel, already the messenger of the Almighty to St. Zachary, father of St. John the Baptist, appeared to Our Blessed Lady and addressed her in those words which all who profess to be Catholics delight to utter: "Hail, full of grace, the Lord is with thee: blessed art thou among women." (Lk 1:28)

St. Luke continues the narration: "Who having heard, was troubled at his saying and thought with herself what manner of salutation this should be." (Lk 1:29)

"And the Angel said to her: 'Fear not, Mary, for thou hast found grace before God. Behold thou shall conceive in thy womb and shall bring forth a Son: and thou shall call his name Jesus.'" (Lk 1:30-31)

"And Mary said to the Angel: 'How shall this be done, because I know not man?' And the Angel answering, said to her: 'The Holy Ghost shall come upon thee, and the power of the Most High shall overshadow thee. And therefore also the Holy [Child] which will be born of thee shall be called the Son of God. And behold thy cousin Elizabeth, she also hath conceived a son in her old age: and this is the sixth month with her that is called barren. Because no word shall be impossible with God.'" (Lk 1:35-37)

"And Mary said: 'Behold the handmaid of the Lord: be it done unto me according to thy word.' And the Angel departed from her." (Lk 1:38)

According to Ven. Mary of Agreda: "At the pronouncing of this *fiat*, so pleasing to God and fortunate for us, four things happened. *First*, the Most Holy Body of Jesus was formed from three drops of blood from the heart of Holy Mary. *Second,* the Most Holy [Human] Soul of Our Lord was created. *Third,* the Soul and Body of Christ were united to form His perfect Humanity. And *fourth,* the Divinity united with the Humanity in the Person of the Word, constituting the Hypostatic Union. And thus was formed Christ, true God and true Man, our Savior and Redeemer. ...

"At the same instant in which the Almighty celebrated the nuptials of the Hypostatic Union in the womb of Most Holy Mary, the heavenly Lady was elevated to the beatific vision and the Divinity was manifested to her clearly and intuitively."[19]

According to Fr. Suarez, on the very day of the Incarnation, Our Lady set out from Nazareth to

---

19. *The Mystical City of God*, Vol. II, *The Incarnation*, pp. 110-112.

visit her cousin St. Elizabeth in the town of Hebron (now called en Karem) in Judea, about 100 miles from Nazareth. [20]According to Ven. Mary of Agreda, the Blessed Mother hastened to visit St. Elizabeth to procure without delay the sanctification of the Precursor of the Incarnate Word, St. John the Baptist, who was yet held prisoner by the bonds of original sin in the womb of Elizabeth.[21]

Her holy spouse St. Joseph accompanied her, and tried to make this difficult trip as comfortable as possible for her. He was, however, unaware of the great and marvelous event that had taken place.

As soon as the holy travelers reached Hebron, the Blessed Virgin entered to meet St. Elizabeth. St. Joseph, according to Jewish tradition, proceeded to pay his respects to St. Zachary. Fr. Vallejo states that theologians agree that St. Joseph, inspired by the Holy Ghost, heard the conversation between the two women, but did not fully understand the great mystery proclaimed.[22] St. Elizabeth greeted Holy Mary with the prophetic utterance: "Blessed art thou amongst women and blessed is the fruit of thy womb" (Lk 1:42).

After those words of praise pronounced by St. Elizabeth, the Blessed Mother, inspired by God, intoned

---

20. Fr. Vallejo, *The Life of St. Joseph*, p. 80.
21. *The Mystical City of God*, Vol. II, *The Incarnation*, p. 162.
22. Fr. Vallejo, *The Life of St. Joseph*, p. 82.

the *Magnificat* as recorded by St. Luke (1:46-55), and described by Ven. Mary of Agreda: [23]

My soul doth magnify the Lord.

And my spirit hath rejoiced in God my Savior.

Because He hath regarded the humility of His handmaid: for behold from henceforth all generations shall call me blessed.

Because He that is mighty hath done great things to me: and holy is His name.

And his mercy is from generation unto generations, to them that fear Him.

He hath showed might in His arm: He hath scattered the proud in the conceit of their heart.

He hath put down the mighty from their seat and hath exalted the humble.

He hath filled the hungry with good things: and the rich He hath sent empty away.

He hath received Israel his servant, being mindful of His mercy.

As He spoke to our fathers: to Abraham and to his seed for ever.

Theologian Abbot Trombelli believes that St. Joseph remained for the three month visitation at the home of St. Zachary and at the end of this period, the Holy Couple returned to their house in Nazareth.[24]

---

23. *The Mystical City of God*, Vol. II, *The Incarnation*, p. 178-179.
24. Fr. Vallejo, *The Life of St. Joseph*, p. 83.

Chapter 8

How St. Joseph Was Informed of the Incarnation

Soon after the return of the Holy Couple to Nazareth and subsequent to a period of calm and joy for St. Joseph, he noted the condition of his spouse, and tribulation and anxiety gripped his heart.

St. Jerome supposes that St. Joseph did not utter a single word, and was convinced of the purity of his Immaculate Spouse, although the mystery of the Incarnation was not fully understood by him. He concluded he must withdraw from Holy Mary without her knowledge. [25]

St. Bernard is of the opinion that St. Joseph wished to depart from her for the same reason that Peter said to Our Lord, "Depart from me, O Lord, for I am a sinner." The Blessed Mother confirmed the opinion of St. Bernard in a revelation to St. Bridget. Our Lady told her: "Joseph, seeing my form expand through the power of the Holy Ghost, was filled with astonishment and admiration. Not entertaining any undue suspicion of me, but remembering the words of the Prophet foretelling that the Son of God should be born of a Virgin, he thought himself unworthy to

---

25. Fr. Vallejo, *The Life of St. Joseph*, p. 87.

serve such a Mother, until the Angel in a dream bode him not fear, but minister to me in charity." [26]

St. Remigius says that Joseph saw that his spouse, who certainly had no relations with mortal man, had nevertheless conceived. He beheld her with child whom he knew to be chaste and he meditated on what he had read in the Prophet Isaias: "A rod shall come forth from the root of Jesse and a flower shall ascend from this root." That is, the God-Man should be born of a daughter of David, the son of Jesse, from whom Joseph's virgin spouse descended. And again: "Behold a virgin shall conceive in her womb" (Is 7:14). Therefore he concluded that his spouse was the object of this prophecy, that in her could be verified this prophecy, given 700 years before with the greatest exactness. [27]

Other ancient writers were in agreement with St. Remigius that Joseph, having read the words of the Prophet Isaias that a virgin descended from David would conceive and bear a Son, was prepared to believe that the prophecy was fulfilled in his spouse.[28]

When Joseph had resolved to withdraw in secret from the Mother of God, he fell into a deep sleep. The Angel of the Lord appeared to him in his sleep

---

26. *Ibid.*, p. 89.
27. *Ibid.,* pp. 89-90.
28. *Ibid.*, p. 90.

saying, "Joseph, son of David, fear not to take unto thee Mary thy wife, for that which is conceived in her is of the Holy Ghost" (Mt 1:20). By means of the apparition of the Angel in his sleep, Joseph was perfectly enlightened. According to Mary of Agreda, the Angel was St. Gabriel.[29]

On receiving this instruction from the Archangel Gabriel, Joseph awoke filled with a holy calm and joy. As a faithful, obedient servant of his Lord, he devoted himself entirely to honoring and serving the Mother of God with the care and respect due her.

St. John Chrysostom comments on how God grants His counsels: soon after St. Joseph became anxious over Mary's condition, He sent an Angel to enlighten him about the Incarnation and banish his fears.[30] Joseph was prompt in obeying the heavenly message and did not doubt as Zachary had done when he received the news that his wife Elizabeth had conceived at an advanced age.

Abbot Trombelli says that Joseph neither asked the Angel for a confirmation of the order, nor of the mystery which he revealed, but immediately did all that was commanded of him.[31]

---

29. *The Mystical City of God*, Vol. II, *The Incarnation*, p. 327.
30. Fr. Vallejo, *The Life of St. Joseph*, p. 94.
31. *Ibid.*

According to the *Mystical City*, it seemed good to Our Lady to console her spouse and therefore, not just to excuse herself, she said to him: "As much as I desired, I could not on my own account give thee any information regarding the sacrament hidden within me by the power of the Almighty, since as His slave, it was my duty to await the manifestation of His holy and perfect will."[32]

* * *

---

32. *The Mystical City of God*, Vol. II, *The Incarnation*, p. 333.

Chapter 9

THE NATIVITY OF OUR LORD JESUS CHRIST

After learning of the Incarnation from the Archangel Gabriel, St. Joseph regarded Blessed Mary more as a sovereign than a spouse. He combined his labors with the continual exercise of heroic virtues, contemplating the fulfillment of the prophecies, and the Messiah who was then under his protection. Although not stated in Sacred Scripture, the consensus of theologians is that, considering the sanctity of Joseph, it is most probable that during the six months he lived in Nazareth before the birth of Jesus, he had frequent apparitions of the Angels as they would descend from Heaven to adore their Creator who then lay hidden in the virginal womb of the Blessed Mother.[33] Certainly the most holy and supernatural event in the life of St. Joseph was the birth of Our Lord Jesus Christ, his earthly Son.

In the last days of these six months when the birth of the God-Man drew near, Joseph, in obedience to the census decree of Caesar, set out with the Blessed Virgin from Nazareth to Bethlehem, the original seat of the royal family of David from which the Holy

---

33. Fr. Vallejo, *The Life of St. Joseph*, p. 109.

Couple descended. The journey was about 96 miles and according to St. Justin, the distance was traveled in five days. Due to the condition of the Mother of God, however, the journey may have been hastened by Mary's choir of Angels.

Since attempts by Joseph to obtain proper lodging were not in the divine plan, he took up abode in a stable within a cave, which would be the place where the birth of the Messiah would occur, as decreed by the Eternal Father. According to Doctors of the Church, when Christ was born the Angels placed Him into the arms of Holy Mary.[34]

Upon the advent, that is, the happy moment when the Infant Jesus was about to come forth, Abbot Trombelli says that St. Joseph left the grotto as dictated by propriety and respect for the Blessed Mother. On hearing the voice of Holy Mary calling him, Joseph returned to the grotto, took Jesus in his arms, and folded Him in the cloak which he wore. A fragment of this mantle or cloak of St. Joseph, according to Pancirollus and Bollandus (both historians and theologians), is preserved in Rome among the relics of the Church of St. Cecilia in Trastevere.[35]

---

34. *Ibid.*, p. 110.
35. *Ibid.*, p. 111.

The description of the birth of Jesus given by Ven. Mary of Agreda[36] is incomparable in its beauty. We transcribe it here:

"The Infant God therefore was brought forth from the virginal chamber unencumbered by any corporeal or material substance foreign to Himself. But He came forth glorious and transfigured, for the Divine and Infinite Wisdom decreed and ordained that in His birth the glory of His most holy soul should overflow and communicate itself to His body, which participated in the gifts of glory [i.e., He had the gift of agility, the glorious gift to move through material obstacles without touching them] in the same way as happened afterwards in His Transfiguration on Mount Tabor in the presence of the three Apostles (Mt 17:2). This miracle [of agility] was not necessary to penetrate the virginal enclosure and leave unimpaired the virginal integrity; for without this Transfiguration, God could have brought this about by other miracles. Thus say the holy Doctors who see no other miracle in this birth than that the Child was born without impairing the virginity of the Mother.

"It was the will of God that the Most Blessed Virgin should look upon the body of her Son, the God-Man, for this first time in a glorified state for

---

36. *The Mystical City of God,* Vol. II, *The Incarnation,* pp. 401-405.

two reasons. The one was in order that by this divine vision, the most prudent Mother should conceive the highest reverence for the Majesty of Him Whom she was to treat as her Son, the true God-Man. Although she had already been informed of His two-fold nature, the Lord nevertheless ordained that by this ocular demonstration, she be filled with new graces corresponding to the divine excellence of her Most Holy Son, and of His majesty and greatness.

"The second reason for this wonder was to reward the fidelity and holiness of the Blessed Mother, for her most pure and chaste eyes, which had turned away from all earthly things for the love of her Most Holy Son, would see Him at His very birth in His glory and thus be rejoiced and rewarded for her loyalty and delicate love.

"The holy evangelist Luke tells us that the Mother Virgin, having brought forth her First-begotten Son, wrapped Him in swathing clothes and placed Him in a manger. He does not say who brought Him to her arms from her virginal womb, for this did not pertain to the purpose of his narrative. But the ministers of this action were the two sovereign Princes, St. Michael and St. Gabriel, who were present in human form assisting at the mystery. At the moment when the Incarnate Word, leaving the virginal chamber by divine power, issued forth to the light, they received

Him in their hands with ineffable reverence. In the same manner as a priest exhibits the Sacred Host to the people for adoration, so these two celestial ministers presented to the Blessed Mother her glorious and refulgent Son. All this happened in a short space of time.

"At the same moment in which the Holy Angels thus presented the Divine Child to His Mother, both Son and Mother looked upon each other, and in this look, she wounded with love the heart of the sweet Infant and was at the same time exalted and transformed in Him. From the arms of the Holy Princess, the Prince of all the Heavens spoke to His Holy Mother: 'Mother become like unto Me, since on this day, in return for the human life which thou hast given Me, I desire to give thee henceforth another more elevated life of grace, assimilating thy life as a mere creature to the likeness of Mine, Who am God and Man.'

"The most prudent Mother answered: *'Trahe me post Te, curremus in odorem unguentorem tuoram'* [Raise me, elevate me, Lord and I will run after Thee in the odor of Thy ointments] (Cant 1:3). ...

"As the Blessed Mary heard these words from the mouth of her most beloved Son, she understood the interior acts of His holiest Soul united with the Divinity, so that, by imitating them, she might become like unto Him. This was the greatest benefit which the most faithful and fortunate Mother received from her Son, true God and Man, not only because it was continued from that day on through all her life, but because it provided her with the living Model from which she molded her life, as faithfully as is possible between a mere creature and Christ, true Man and God.

"At the same time, the heavenly Lady perceived and felt the presence of the Most Holy Trinity, and she heard the voice of the Eternal Father saying, 'This is my beloved Son, in whom I am greatly pleased and delighted' (Mt 17:5).

"The most prudent Mother answered: 'Eternal Father and exalted God, Lord and Creator of the universe, give me anew Thy permission and benediction to receive in my arms the Desired of nations (Ag 2:8), and teach me to fulfill as Thy unworthy Mother and lowly slave, Thy holy will.' Immediately she heard a voice, which said: 'Receive thy Only-begotten Son, imitate Him and rear Him; and remember that thou must sacrifice Him when I shall request it of thee.'

"The blessed Mother answered: 'Behold the creature of Thy divine hands, adorn me with Thy grace so that Thy Son and my God receive me for His slave, so that with the aid of Thy great power, I can be faithful in His service; and do Thou count it no presumption in Thy insignificant creature that she bear in her arms and nourish at her breast her own Lord and Creator.'

"After this interchange of words, so full of mysteries, the Infant God suspended the miracle of His Transfiguration, and He inaugurated another miracle, suspending the effects of glory in His Most Holy Body, confining them solely to His Soul. He now assumed the appearance of one capable of suffering. In this form, the most pure Mother now saw Him and, remaining in a kneeling position and adoring Him, with profound humility and reverence, she received Him in her arms from the hands of the Holy Angels.

"Then, the most prudent Mother turned toward the Eternal Father to offer up to Him His Onlybegotten, saying: 'Exalted Creator of the entire universe, here is the altar and the sacrifice acceptable in Thy eyes (Malach 3:4). From this hour on, O Lord, look upon the human race with mercy, and inasmuch as we have deserved Thy anger, it is now time that Thou be appeased in Thy Son and mine. Let Thy justice now come to rest, and let Thy mercy be exalted; for on this account the Word has clothed itself with flesh like unto sinful flesh (Rom 8: 3) and become a Brother of mortals and sinners (Phil 2:7).'"

It seems appropriate to express certain thoughts on the Nativity of Our Lord and Savior Jesus Christ and the reception such a sublime revelation has received in the last years.

It is painful to see how the Progressivists often scorn the magnificent presentation of the Ven. Mary of Agreda on the birth of Jesus. Sadly, even some traditionalist Catholics would hold the account in doubt because such is not in Sacred Scripture.

We are blessed with gifts from Heaven given to us through great Saints and approved mystics to enhance, enlighten and edify our knowledge of the supernatural. Nonetheless, there are those who, like the Protestants and the Progressivists, would state that Christ was unaware of His Divinity and mission until the time of His public life, which is an absurdity.

Others would strictly interpret the few words of Sacred Scripture on the early life of Christ, that is, that He grew in wisdom and knowledge (Lk 2:52). Many theologians, including Fr. Suarez, state that by this we understand He grew in wisdom and knowledge in the eyes of the world; however, as God-Man, even as an Infant the understanding of His Divinity was complete.

The sense of probability dictates that His Transfiguration at His Birth by the Eternal Father and His discourse with the Blessed Mother were events appropriate to express the fullness of His Divinity. Indeed, since Our Lord was transfigured by the Eternal Father at His baptism, and at Mount Tabor before His Passion and death, it seems reasonable that the Eternal Father would also have glorified Him at His birth. The revelation of Ven. Mary of Agreda is highly probable and credible.

In the Garden of Gethsemane, Christ offered the enormity of the suffering He was about to undergo to the Father. That he disbanded His Divinity in the Agony in the Garden is clear from the words, "My soul is sorrowful unto death," and "Father, if it be possible, let this chalice pass from Me." In the *Transfixion*, Ven. Mary of Agreda says, "The Lord permitted this sorrow to reach the highest degree both naturally and miraculously possible in His Sacred Humanity."[37]

The Divinity of Jesus Christ always overshadowed His Sacred Humanity. Only in the Agony in the Garden of Gethsemane did He disband His Divinity to suffer fully in His Humanity at the sight of the sins of the world, His own upcoming Passion and Crucifixion, and the suffering of His Sorrowful Mother.

By contrast, Our Lord used His Divinity, which deified His Most Holy Humanity by its Hypostatic Union, to enable his Humanity to suffer physically to

---

37. *The Mystical City of God,* Vol. III, *The Transfixion,* pp. 478-479.

extremes far beyond human comprehension and capability in His Passion and Crucifixion. The above revelations were stressed by Ven. Mary of Agreda. [38]

Mankind should be deeply grateful to the Blessed Mother for the marvelous revelations she made to Ven. Mary of Agreda concerning the Nativity of Our Lord and His Agony, Passion and Death, which have greatly enhanced our knowledge of these sacred mysteries.

* * *

---

38. *Ibid.*, p. 642.

Chapter 10

THE CIRCUMCISION OF THE INFANT JESUS AND HIS PRESENTATION IN THE TEMPLE

The law of circumcision, to be observed on the eighth day after birth, was a religious ceremony introduced by order of the God of Israel in order to distinguish the sons of Abraham, Isaac and Jacob from the rest of the earthly nations. By this sign, the Hebrews were made members of the Chosen People. The practice of this rite dated from the time of Moses and is in the Mosaic Law. In obedience to this law, the Infant Jesus was circumcised because He wished to show the sons of Judah and in them, the whole world, that He came to fulfill the law entirely before abrogating it and becoming the author of the New Testament.

Who administered the rite is a matter of some controversy, with different opinions being expressed by St. Jerome, St. Bernard and Abbot Trombelli.[39] On the day that the rite was carried out, the name of the infant was given according to Hebrew custom. The Holy Couple had a heavenly revelation that the name should be Jesus, signifying Savior of the human race. This signification gave great joy to the hearts

---

39. Fr. Vallejo, *The Life of St. Joseph*, pp. 114-115.

of St. Joseph and Holy Mary, who nonetheless felt an intense sorrow at the carrying out of this painful ceremony, which took place in the stable and grotto of Bethlehem.[40] Sacred Scripture proclaims the name of Jesus: "Thou shall call his name Jesus for He shall save the people from their sins" (Mt 1:21); "Behold thou shall conceive in thy womb and shall bring forth a Son and thou shall call His name Jesus" (Lk 1:31).

A beautiful revelation of this event is given by Ven. Mary of Agreda.[41] A few selected citations will be presented to enlighten the reader as to what occurred:

"Our great Queen, not on account of any apprehension of danger but because of the dignity of the Child, also wished a priest to administer this rite to Him; and therefore she sent her most fortunate spouse to Bethlehem to call the priest of that town. The priest came to the gates or cave of the Nativity, where the Incarnate Word, resting in the arms of his Virgin Mother, awaited him. With the priest came also two other officials, who were to render such assistance as was customary at the performance of the rite. The rudeness of the dwelling at first astonished and somewhat disconcerted the priest.

---

40. *Ibid.*, p. 116
41. *The Mystical City of God*, Vol. II, *The Incarnation*, pp. 446-451.

Chapter 10

"When the priest looked upon the face of Mary and of the Child in her arms, he was filled with great devotion and tenderness, wondering at the contrast exhibited amid such poverty and in a place so lowly and despised. And when he proceeded to touch the divine flesh of the Infant, he was renovated by a secret influence which sanctified and perfected him; it gave him a new existence in grace, and raised him up to a state of holiness very pleasing to the most high Lord. ...

"In order to show as much exterior reverence for the sacred rite of circumcision as was possible in that place, St. Joseph lighted two wax candles. The priest requested the Virgin Mother to consign the Child to the arms of the two assistants and withdraw for a short time in order not to be obliged to witness the sacrifice.

"This command caused some hesitation in the great Lady for her humility and spirit of obedience inclined her to obey the priest, while on the other hand, she was withheld by her love and reverence for her Only-begotten. In order not to fail against either of these virtues, she humbly requested to be allowed to remain, saying that she desired to be present at the performance of this rite, since she held it in great esteem, and that she would have courage to hold her Son in her arms, as she wished not to leave Him alone on such an occasion. All that she would ask would be that the circumcision be performed with as much tenderness as possible on account of the delicacy of the Child.

"The priest promised to fulfill her request, and permitted the Child to be held in the arms of His Mother for fulfilling the mystery. Thus she became the sacred altar on which the truths typified in the ancient sacrifice became a reality (Heb 9:6). And she herself offered up this new morning's sacrifice in her own arms in order that it might be acceptable to the Eternal Father in all particulars. ...

"While holding the Child in her hands, she placed the towel so that the relics and the blood of the circumcision would fall upon it. The priest thereupon proceeded to his duty and circumcised the Child, the true God and Man. At the same time the Son of God, with immeasurable love, offered up to the Eternal Father three sacrifices of so great value that each one would have been sufficient for the Redemption of a thousand worlds.

"The *first* was that He, being innocent and the Son of the true God, assumed the condition of a sinner (Phil 2:7) by submitting Himself to a rite instituted as a remedy for original sin and to a law not binding on Him (II Cor 5:21). The *second* was His willingness to suffer the pains of circumcision, which He felt as a true and perfect Man. The *third* was the most ardent love with which He began to shed His Blood for the human race, giving thanks to the Eternal Father for having given Him a human nature capable of suffering for His exaltation and glory. ...

"This prayerful sacrifice of Jesus Our Savior, the Father accepted, and, according to our way of speaking, He began to declare Himself satisfied and compensated for the indebtedness of humanity. The Incarnate Word offered these first fruits of His Blood as pledges that He would give all His Blood in order to consummate the Redemption and extinguish the debt of the sons of Adam. ...

"In the meanwhile the priest asked the parents what name they wished to give to the Child in circumcision. The great Lady, always attentive to honor her spouse, asked St. Joseph to speak the name. St. Joseph turned toward her in like reverence and gave her to understand that he thought it proper that this sweet name should first flow from her mouth. Therefore, by divine intervention, both Mary and Joseph said at the same time: 'Jesus is His name.' The priest answered: 'The parents are unanimously agreed, and great is the name which they give to the Child.'

"Thereupon he inscribed it in the tablet or register of names of the rest of the children. While writing it, the priest felt great interior movements, so that he shed copious tears. And wondering at what he felt yet not being able to account for it, he said: 'I am convinced that this Child is to be a great Prophet of the Lord. Have great care in raising Him, and tell me in what ways I can relieve your needs.' Most Holy Mary and Joseph answered the priest with humble gratitude and dismissed him after offering him the gift of some candles and other articles."

As St. Luke relates (2:22), when the period of 40 days had elapsed according to the Law of Moses (Ex 13), every mother was required to purify herself at the Temple, and the parents to offer their child to the Lord. Because she did not have original sin, Our Lady was above the Old Law. Our Lord, who is God, also was not subject to the Law so, in principle, neither of them was obliged to go. But she wanted to do so out of respect for the Judaic Law and to demonstrate her humility.

Ven. Mary of Agreda gives this account of the arrival of the Holy Family into Jerusalem:

"During the journey of Our Lady with the Infant God, it happened that in Jerusalem Simeon the high priest was enlightened by the Holy Ghost concerning the coming of the Incarnate Word and His presentation in the Temple in the arms of His Mother. The same revelation was given to the holy widow Anna, and she was also informed of the poverty and suffering of St. Joseph and the most pure Lady on their way to Jerusalem.

"These two holy persons, immediately conferring with each other about their revelations and enlightenments, called the chief procurator of the temporal affairs of the Temple and, describing to him the signs whereby he should recognize the holy Travelers, they ordered him to proceed to the gate leading out to Bethlehem and receive them into his house with all benevolence and hospitality. This the procurator did, and thus the Queen and her spouse were much relieved, since they had been anxious about finding a proper lodging for the Divine Infant. Leaving them well provided in his house, the fortunate host returned in order to report to the high priest." [42]

On the following day, St. Joseph and Holy Mary entered the Temple with the Infant Jesus. The holy, elderly priest Simeon came forward to greet them. Filled with faith and heavenly light, Simeon greeted the Redeemer of his people. Previously this old high priest had received an answer from Heaven regarding his desire to see the Savior, as related by Luke: "And he had received an answer from the Holy Ghost, that he should not see death before he had seen the Christ of the Lord" (2:26).

Inspired from on high, Simeon took the Child in his arms and giving thanks to the Almighty, he burst

---

42. *The Mystical City of God*, Vol. II, *The Incarnation*, p. 501.

forth with the sublime words, *Nunc dimittis servum tuum Domine* ... "Now Thou dost dismiss Thy servant in peace, O Lord, according to Thy word. Because my eyes have seen my salvation, which Thou hast prepared before the face of all peoples, a Light to the revelation of the Gentiles and the glory of Thy people Israel." [43]

Then, turning toward the Blessed Mother, he uttered this prophecy: "Behold this Child is set for the fall and for the resurrection of many in Israel, and for a sign which shall be contradicted." [44]

"A most fatal day shall come for Jerusalem when this Child shall be sentenced to a most ignominious death. And the execution of this sentence, cruel beyond the power of imagination, will be, O Mary, a sword to pierce thy soul." [45]

St. Luke states: "And thy own soul a sword shall pierce that out of many hearts thoughts may be revealed." [46]

It is reported by several of the ancient writers that Simeon, on receiving Jesus in his arms, recovered his sight.

---

43. Lk 2:29-32.
44. Lk 2:34
45. Fr. Vallejo, *The Life of St. Joseph*, p. 127.
46. Lk 2:35.

A brief commentary on this chapter is now presented. As a divine prelude to His Passion and Death, Jesus shed His Precious Blood at the Jewish rite of circumcision. As Ven. Mary of Agreda has stated, this alone would have sufficed for the salvation of a thousand worlds.

The Triune God, foreseeing the great apostasy in His Church, the perversion in His clergy, the massive number of abortions and a world permeated with evil, decreed that His Only-begotten Son shed all of His Precious Blood at His Passion, Crucifixion and Death on the Cross. When Longinus pierced His Sacred Heart, the sacrifice was consummated.

As stated above, Simeon prophesized at the Presentation of the Infant Jesus in the Temple that this Child would be sentenced to an ignominious death and that the soul of Holy Mary would be pierced.

Most Sorrowful and Immaculate Heart of Mary, pray for us.

* * *

Chapter 11

THE FLIGHT INTO EGYPT, THE MASSACRE OF THE HOLY INNOCENTS, AND THE RETURN TO NAZARETH

Prior to the Presentation of Our Lord in the Temple, the Three Magi had arrived at the grotto and adored the Newborn King, as St. Matthew relates (2:10-11). On route to the grotto in Bethlehem, the Wise Men had been received by Herod in Jerusalem. Herod told the Magi to return and report to him where the expected Messiah was so that he could also adore Him. The Magi were warned in dreams of Herod's evil designs for the Child and decided to return home by a different route to thwart them (Mt 2:12).

As soon as he realized that the Wise Men had returned to Arabia bypassing Jerusalem, Herod was convinced that the King of the Jews had been born. To protect his rights to the throne in Judea, he thereupon planned to issue one of the cruelest orders ever witnessed in History. His bloody mandate would call for the murder of every male child born in Bethlehem and the surrounding area during the last two years, the latter provision made in case the Savior might have been born before the appearance of the star that guided the Magi. [47]

---

47. *The Mystical City of God*, Vol. II, *The Incarnation*, pp. 575-576.

The Holy Family was still in Jerusalem[48] when one night while St. Joseph slept, an Angel of the Lord appeared to him, telling him of Herod's insidious plan and warning him to flee to Egypt with the Infant Jesus and His Blessed Mother. Without waiting for the day to dawn, St. Joseph obeyed the order from Heaven. St. John Chrysostom praises his prompt response in these words: "For Joseph was a faithful man, nor did he ask the time of his return. He is not slothful, but obeys, and bears all temptations with joy."[49]

The Gospels do not tell why Heaven ordered St. Joseph to flee to Egypt, and not to some other place. It is proposed by historians that in the surrounding countries, there was much hatred of the Jews, but in Egypt the Jews were treated kindly and with regard.[50]

The Holy Family made the journey to Egypt through the rugged Negev desert and the Sinai, a distance of over 400 miles, accompanied by the Angelic legions of the Holy Mary. The flight into Egypt took place in the month of February, at the height of winter, only six days after the Presentation in the Temple

---

48. The Holy Family planned to stay nine days in Jerusalem. Ater five days, the Angel instructed St. Joseph to flee into Egypt. *Ibid.*, pp. 519-521.

49. St. John Chrysostom, *Hom.* VIII.

50. Fr. Vallejo, *The Life of St. Joseph,* p. 132.

and the Purification. Through the Angels who accompanied the Holy Family on the trip, Divine Providence protected them against the severity of the weather, although they still endured the sufferings of travel.

A beautiful event recorded by biblical scholars occurred as the Holy Family proceeded on their journey to Egypt. They happened on a camp of robbers who at first seemed hostile. But on seeing the Holy Family, they showed reverence toward them. Mary requested a large container filled with water to bathe the Infant Jesus. Realizing that Jesus was no ordinary Infant, the wife of one of the robbers requested that she be allowed to bathe her disfigured leprous three-year-old son in the same water. The child was instantly cured with no sign of this horrible disease.

Thirty-three years later, Dismas, the child cured of leprosy, said to the crucified Jesus on Calvary: "Lord, remember me when Thou come into Thy Kingdom." And Our Lord said to him, "Amen, I say to thee, this day thou shall be with me in paradise" (Lk 23:43).

St. Thomas Aquinas concurs with early historians and theologians that St. Joseph took Holy Mary and the Infant Jesus to Heliopolis, a large city in Northern Egypt.[51] Heliopolis took its name, the City of the

---

51. *Ibid.*, p. 137.

Sun, from an image of that celestial body which was venerated there, thus demonstrating the idolatry prevalent in this superstitious nation. Fr. Suarez relates that many Jews dwelt in Heliopolis where they had a magnificent synagogue.[52]

Ven. Mary of Agreda provides more details about the story of the Holy Family in Egypt. Her words will be paraphrased in the rest of this section.[53]

When the Infant Jesus arrived in Heliopolis with His Holy Mother and St. Joseph, large numbers of idols, temples, and altars to the demons fell to the ground, shattered to dust with a great crashing noise. The inhabitants were confused and astonished by the suddenness of this destruction.

As the Blessed Mother instructed, inspired and calmed the people, they viewed her with love and esteem. Under the guidance of her Divine Son, the Blessed Mother instructed and converted a great multitude of the Egyptians during the seven-year sojourn of the Holy Family in this pagan country. Her Divine Son Jesus allowed Holy Mary to effect miraculous cures of the sick throughout Heliopolis and

---

52. *Ibid.*

53. *The Mystical City of God*, Vol. II, *The Incarnation*, in Chapters XXVI, XXVII, XXIX and XXX.

surrounding areas. In essence, the Holy Family sanctified a considerable part of pagan Egypt.

Meanwhile, in Judea, Herod's fury increased and after contemplating and carefully planning his massacre of the Holy Innocents, he issued the edict mandating the slaughter. By divine enlightenment, Holy Mary had a clear picture of the horror that was to take place in Bethlehem and surrounding regions. She was greatly concerned about St. Elizabeth and John the Baptist. She was given to know that an Angel had instructed St. Elizabeth to flee into the desert with the Precursor of Jesus. Divine Providence protected and sustained them during their hardships in the desert. When the hour of the death of St. Elizabeth arrived, Mary sent many of her Angels to assist her and St. John, who was then four-years-old.

In Heliopolis, the Infant Jesus passed his first year, and the Blessed Mother made for Him the seamless tunic which was to clothe Him until the executioners tore it off Him before the cruel scourging at the pillar. This garment – so revered throughout History – continually grew with Him, adjusting perfectly to His Sacred Body. The same happened with the sandals and the undergarment which Mary made for Him. These garments never lost their newness or became soiled, even on the many occasions when at a tender age Jesus perspired blood, in anticipation of the copious perspiring of Precious Blood that He would shed at age 33 in the Garden of Gethsemane.

The Child Jesus came to be esteemed and loved by all who knew Him. At age six, He began to visit and heal the sick in hospitals and instill into their minds knowledge of the true God and sorrow for their sins without their knowing how these blessings came to them. When He reached the end of His seventh year in Egypt, to fulfill the prophecies, the Holy Family returned to Nazareth. Neither Jesus nor his Blessed Mother informed Joseph of the heavenly mandate they had received to return to Nazareth, but an Angel of the Lord revealed this to him in his sleep, as related by Matthew (2:19).

Avoiding the road through Jerusalem, the Holy Family returned to Nazareth via Gaza along the Mediterranean Sea to Mount Carmel, where they stopped at the cave of Elias. Then they proceeded west through the Valley of Megiddo to the Holy House in Nazareth. The return trip was almost 600 miles, but throughout the trip the Holy Family was accompanied by the Blessed Virgin's legion of Angels.

* * *

Chapter 12

ST. JOSEPH'S LIFE AT NAZARETH AND THE FINDING OF THE CHILD JESUS IN THE TEMPLE

After the return from Egypt, little is recorded in Sacred History concerning the life of St. Joseph. St. Luke tells us: "And his parents went every year to Jerusalem, at the solemn day of the Pasch" (2:41). At the time of St. Joseph, the place appointed for fulfillment of the Law was the magnificent Temple in Jerusalem. These pilgrimages to the Temple before Jesus attained the age of twelve comprise the written history of St. Joseph's life for that time period. Doctors and Saints of the Church have conjectured, however, that the virtue he practiced, enlightened by the example of the Child Jesus and His Holy Mother and his total obedience to God's orders, brought St. Joseph to great heights of sanctity.[54]

Historians are of the opinion that the Tetrarch of Galilee, Herod Antipas, son of King Herod, was no longer seeking the Jewish Messiah so that St. Joseph's fear to make the pilgrimages to Jerusalem was alleviated.[55] St. Luke goes on to record a specific incident regarding the pilgrimage the Blessed

---

54. Fr. Vallejo, *The Life of St. Joseph,* p. 153.
55. *Ibid.,* pp. 153-154.

Mother and St. Joseph made when Jesus was 12-years-old (2: 42-51). Having fulfilled the customs of the feast, Mary and Joseph returned to Nazareth, but unknown to his parents, Jesus remained in Jerusalem. After a day's journey, they thought Him to be with relatives and friends. Not finding Him, however, they returned to Jerusalem. After three days of searching, they found Him in the Temple with the Jewish doctors and priests. All that heard Jesus were amazed at His wisdom and knowledge.

Holy Mary said to Jesus: "Son, why hast Thou done so to us? Behold Thy father and I have sought Thee sorrowing." (Lk 2:48)

And He said to them: "How is it that you sought me? Did you not know that I must be about my Father's business?" (Lk 2:49)

Then He returned with them to Nazareth and was subject to them.

The joy of the Blessed Virgin in finding the Child Jesus in the Temple has been a subject of devout meditation and is the Fifth Joyful Mystery which the faithful delight to contemplate in the Rosary. The consolation and joy of Holy Mary was shared to the fullest extent by St. Joseph.

According to St. Jerome,[56] on the return from Jerusalem, St. Joseph lived with utmost happiness in the presence of Jesus and His Holy Mother. There is, however, no recorded account about the life of St. Joseph in the Holy House of Nazareth after this description of the finding of Jesus in the Temple discoursing with the doctors. Of importance are the brief words of St. Luke (2:51), *"Subditus illis"* [He was subject to them], which means that the Divine Son, after completing His twelfth year, continued to live under the authority of St. Joseph and Holy Mary.

St. Justin states that St. Joseph continued his trade as carpenter in Nazareth and that Jesus assisted him, learning from his foster-father the art of carpentry.[57] The interior life of St. Joseph is obscure historically. We have, however, that brief description of Joseph as "being a just man" (Mt:1:19) in Scripture, That magnificent word "just" can thus effectively describe the enormity of sanctity achieved by St. Joseph.

Ven. Mary of Agreda answers a question often speculated upon about the nature of the meeting of the Child Jesus with the Jewish doctors. On the day of this meeting, the subject under discussion was

---

56. *Ibid.*, p. 161.
57. *Ibid.,* p. 162.

a doubtful point in Sacred Scripture about the coming of the Messiah. The Child Jesus presented Himself to the rabbis as a humble disciple, giving them to understand that He wished to hear their discussion on the coming of the Messiah. The discourse of Jesus with them was lengthy, with this as the crux of His argument:

"Accordingly, when we wish to understand how His first coming shall happen in power and majesty, or as David says, that He shall reign from sea to sea, that in His coming He shall be glorious as said by the other Prophets: all this should not be interpreted as referring to His visible and terrestrial sovereignty, with all its outward show of pomp and majesty; but rather should be interpreted as referring to a new spiritual reign that He shall found in a new Church which shall extend over all the earth with majesty, power, and riches of grace and virtue in opposition to the Devil. By this interpretation the whole Scripture becomes clear; otherwise the parts cannot be in harmony.

"That the people of the Jews are under the dominion of the Romans and are in no condition to restore their sovereignty is not a proof that the Messiah did not come, but on the contrary, it is an infallible sign that He has already come into the world. For our Patriarch Jacob has pointed out this very sign for the guidance of his posterity, commanding them to expect the Messiah when they would see the tribe of Judah deprived of the scepter and sovereignty of Israel (Gen 49:10)."[58]

Other Old Testament references were cited by the Child Jesus as proof that the Messiah was in their midst. Clearly, the Child Jesus lucidly explained to the Jewish rabbis that the Messiah was not to be a king with armies to conquer nations by the sword, but rather Christ the King to conquer souls by means of the Holy Catholic Church throughout the world.

The Child Jesus also reminded the scribes and rabbis of the prophecies already fulfilled, e.g. the newborn Redeemer at Bethlehem, the Magi led by the star to adore Him, the slaughter of the Holy Innocents, and many other things.[59] All who heard Jesus were astonished at the arguments He presented, but as we know, such were not accepted then and are rejected to this day.

* * *

---

58. *The Mystical City of God,* Vol. III, *The Transfixion,* pp. 51-53.
59. *Ibid.,* p. 52.

Chapter 13

THE SUFFERING AND DEATH OF ST. JOSEPH AND EVIDENCE OF HIS ASSUMPTION INTO HEAVEN

Offering insight into the final days of St. Joseph, Ven. Mary of Agreda gives a beautiful description in *The Mystical City of God, The Transfixion,* chapters XIII, XV and XVI. A summary of these chapters will be presented in the following five paragraphs.

While Our Lady endured great physical and mental suffering during the Passion of her Divine Son, the Dormition of the Blessed Mother occurred peacefully and without physical suffering. St. Joseph, however, was led along the Way of the Cross by Our Lord before his death, even though he was loved by Jesus above all the sons of men.

In the last years of his life, St. Joseph was afflicted with multiple illnesses which caused him much suffering and weakness. Holy Mary was aware of the severity of his suffering and contemplated the sincerity and purity of his soul. She often supplicated her Son to alleviate St. Joseph's suffering, and He would comply with her requests. Mary constantly consoled and comforted St. Joseph in the days of his final agony.

At the request of Mary to her Divine Son, for nine days and nights before the death of St. Joseph he uninterruptedly enjoyed the company and attendance of Holy Mary and Jesus. By the command of Jesus, the Angels provided celestial music and the dwelling was filled with the sweetest fragrance, which greatly comforted St. Joseph. The day before he died, St. Joseph was wholly inflamed with heavenly love and remained in an ecstasy for 24 hours, during which time great knowledge of the Divinity was revealed to him.

Right before his death St. Joseph requested his blessed spouse to give him her blessing, but Holy Mary requested her Divine Son to bless him in her stead. Jesus complied with her wish. Mary then requested the blessing of her spouse St. Joseph, which he gave her.

After St. Joseph died, the Blessed Mother began to prepare his body according to Jewish custom. No other hands touched him other than her own and those of the Angels who assisted her in human form. The body of St. Joseph was enveloped in a wonderful light, and only his face could be seen. Accompanied by Jesus and the Angels, the sacred body of St. Joseph was borne to the common burying site in Nazareth.

Because of the holy and blessed death of St. Joseph, the Church has made him patron of a happy death. St. Alphonsus Liguori affirms the importance of praying to St. Joseph for a good death: "Since we all must die, we should cherish a special devotion to St. Joseph, that he may obtain for us a happy death. All Catholics regard him as the advocate of the dying who had honored him during their lives, and they do so for three reasons:

"*First*, because Jesus Christ loved him not only as a friend, but as a father, and on this account his mediation is far more efficacious than that of any other Saint. *Second*, because St. Joseph has obtained special power against the evil spirits, who tempt us with redoubled vigor at the hour of death. *Third*, the assistance given St. Joseph at his death by Jesus and Mary obtained for him the right to secure a holy and peaceful death for his servants. Hence, if they invoke him at the hour of death he will not only help them, but he will also obtain for them the assistance of Jesus and Mary."

St. Alphonsus also relates what St. Bernard says of the power that St. Joseph exercises in distributing graces to those who put their confidence in him: "There are Saints who have the power of protecting us in certain circumstances, but it has been granted to St. Joseph to succor us in every kind of necessity and defend all who fly to him with sentiments of piety." [60]

St. Teresa of Avila stands out among the many great saints greatly devoted to St. Joseph. The love that St. Teresa bore the spouse of Holy Mary and her zeal in promoting his glory was accompanied by signal graces and miracles through his intercession. As cited by Fr. Elias of Saint Teresa, "So many were the benefits both temporal and spiritual which our holy Mother St. Teresa received through St. Joseph, that in her alone we have an image of all favors that can be desired." [61]

St. Teresa herself says, "It seems that God has granted to other saints to aid us only in certain necessities, but we will find by experience that St. Joseph can aid us in all." Her statement confirms the testimony of St. Bernard.

St. Joseph gave miraculous aid to St. Teresa, curing her on several occasions of terminal diseases. He saved her and her nuns from an accident on a precipice where instant death seemed a certainty. When she began her reform, he helped her not only to erect many new convents, but to save many which had gone hopelessly astray.[62]

---

60. Fr. Vallejo, *The Life of St. Joseph*, p. 341.
61. *Ibid.*, p. 306.
62. *Ibid.*, p. 307.

In her *Autobiography*, St. Teresa states: "Would that I could persuade all men to be devoted to this glorious Saint [St. Joseph], for I know by long experience what blessings he can obtain for us from God. I have never known anyone who was truly devoted to him and honored him by particular services who did not advance greatly in virtue: for he helps in a special way those souls who commend themselves to him. It is now very many years since I began asking him for something on his feast, and I have always received it. If the petition was in any way amiss, he rectified it for my greater good." [63]

She suggests that those who do not believe her words make the trial for themselves. Then they will find out by experience the great good that results from commending themselves to this glorious Patriarch and in being devoted to him.

Our Lady herself affirmed the intercessory power of her spouse in words to Ven. Mary of Agreda: "On the Day of Judgment, the condemned will weep bitterly for not having realized how powerful and efficacious a means of salvation they might have had in the intercession of St. Joseph, and for not having done their utmost to gain the friendship of the Eternal Judge." [64]

---

63. *Autobiography*, Chap. VI, pp. 11-12.
64. *The Mystical City of God,* Vol. III, *The Transfixion,* p. 167.

The great St. Joseph reached an age of 60 years and a few days. Jesus was 30-years-old at his death, and was preparing to enter His public life to preach the Gospel. After his death, St. Joseph went to Limbo, awaiting there the Redemption his Son would accomplish.

While describing the death of St. Joseph, an important attribute of the Blessed Mother is revealed in *The Mystical City*.[65] The wonderful beauty and vitality of Mary that she had attained at the age of 33 remained unchanged with time. When she reached her 70th year at the time of her Dormition and subsequent Assumption into Heaven, her virginal body remained as it was at age 33. With her infused knowledge of the Divinity, the Virgin Mary had guided her Divine Son's Church and the Apostles for about 23 years after His death on the Cross.

St. Matthew reports this after Our Lord's death: "And the graves were opened; and many bodies of the Saints that had slept arose. And coming out of the tombs after His Resurrection, came into the holy city and appeared to many" (27:52-53).

These Saints, who were liberated from Limbo after His death, appeared in Jerusalem after His Res-

---

65. *Ibid.,* p. 133.

urrection and rose with Him to Heaven, according to many interpreters.

While there is no unanimity among these interpreters regarding the Saints who were raised from the dead, there are, however, many who consider that the body of St. Joseph, so exalted in dignity and favor, was united in glory with his soul in Heaven.

The resurrection of St. Joseph, according to Abbot Trombelli, was a certainty. The reason he gives for this was that St. Joseph's exalted presence was a source of great consolation and joy to his Immaculate Spouse. [66]

On this topic, St. Thomas Aquinas speaks as follows: "It may be asked what became of those who rose with Our Lord? For we must believe that they returned to life to be witnesses of Christ's Resurrection. Some think that they died again, relapsing into their former dust. But these authors are unworthy of credit, for it would be a greater torture for those Saints to die a second time, than not to have been raised to life. We must then believe without further examination that the Saints who rose with Jesus ascended with Him to Heaven." [67]

---

66. Fr. Vallejo, *The Life of St. Joseph*, p. 180.
67. *Ibid.*

In addition to these words of the Angelic Doctor, St. Joseph has in favor of his permanent resurrection the fact that neither on the spot where his tomb is said to have been nor in any part of the world is there a known relic of St. Joseph's body. This, despite the fact that we know by human investigation or divine revelations that relics have been found of the bodies of St. Anne, St. Joachim, St. John the Baptist and the Apostles.

St. Francis de Sales writes, "The glorious Patriarch had earned a tremendous reward in Heaven for all that he had done for the Son, preparing the way for His heavenly mission ... How could Jesus deny His gift of eternal bliss to the person whom He had obeyed so faithfully on earth? I believe that on seeing Jesus, Joseph would have told Him, 'My Lord, remember that when You came down from Heaven I received You into my family and my home. When You appeared on earth, it was I who took You tenderly into my arms. Now take me into Yours. Just as I once fed You and looked after You on earth, be so kind now as to lead me to eternal life.'" [68]

---

68. Sermon on St. Joseph, 7, in F. Fernandez, *In Conversation with God* (Scepter Publishers, 1992), p. 160.

69. Fr. Vallejo, *The Life of St. Joseph,* p. 181.

It is the pious belief of St. Bernardine of Sienna that the Holy Family who lived in the same union and charity on earth live body and soul in heavenly glory according to the rule of the Apostle St. Paul,[69] who says that the companions of Christ in consolation shall be those who shared His tribulations (II Cor 1:7).

St. Bernardine preached that although it is not a defined dogma, we are free to believe that Jesus honored His adopted father in the same way as he has honored His Blessed Mother. He states, "In the same way that Mary was assumed into Heaven, it is thought that Jesus deigned to glorify Joseph on the day of the Resurrection. In this way, all of the Holy Family – Jesus, Mary and Joseph – who lived together on earth, would reign together in Heaven."[70]

Confirming this opinion, Fr. Bernardine de Bustos joyfully states that while St. Bernardine of Sienna was preaching in Padua that St. Joseph was body and soul in Heaven, a large crucifix of gold brilliant with heavenly light appeared above his head. By this prodigy, Heaven wished to attest the truth of what the illustrious orator St. Bernardine was pronouncing concerning the holy spouse of the Our Lady and father of Our Lord and Savior Jesus Christ.[71]

---

70. *Homily 3 on St. Joseph*, in Fernandez, *ibid.,* p. 161.
71. Fr. Vallejo, *The Life of St. Joseph*, pp.181-82.

Numerous theologians and historians have stated that St. Joseph rose and ascended with Our Lord into Heaven, and this has been believed by many of the faithful over the years. [72]

What joy there must have been in Heaven, when after 23 more years in guiding her Divine Son's Church, Holy Mary was assumed into Heaven and finally united with her beloved Jesus the God-Man and her glorious spouse St. Joseph.

*

St. Joseph, Patron of the Universal Church, intercede with your Immaculate Spouse and your Divine Son who loved you so dearly to end the apostasy that engulfs His Holy Church and deign to restore her to her former beauty.

* * *

---

72. *Ibid.*, p. 182.

Appendix 1

Quotes in Holy Scripture regarding St. Joseph [73]

1. Events Recorded in the Gospels

• The book of the generation of Jesus Christ, the Son of David, the son of Abraham. Abraham begot Issac. And Nathan begot Jacob. And Jacob begot Joseph, the husband of Mary, of whom was born Jesus, who is called Christ. (Mt: 1:1-2, 15-16)

• And Joseph, rising up from sleep, did as the Angel of the Lord had commanded him, and took unto him his wife. (Mt 1:24)

• The Angel Gabriel was sent from God to a virgin espoused to a man whose name was Joseph, of the house of David. (Lk 1: 26-27)

• When his mother was espoused to Joseph. before they came together, she was found with Child of the Holy Ghost. (Mt 1:18)

• Whereupon Joseph her husband, being a just man, and not willing publicly to expose her, was minded to put her away privately. (Mt 1:19)

• But while he thought on these things, behold the Angel of the Lord appeared to him in his sleep, saying;

---

73. Kenelm Vaugham and Newton Thomson S.T.D., *Scripture by Topic* (Fort Collins, CO: Roman Catholic Books, 1943), pp. 86-88.

Joseph, son of David, fear not to take unto thee Mary thy wife, for that which is conceived in her is of the Holy Ghost. (Mt 1:20)

- They wondered at the words of grace that proceeded from his mouth, and they said: Is not this the son of Joseph? (Lk 4:22)
- Philip findeth Nathanael, and saith to him: We have found Him of whom Moses in the Law and the Prophets did write, Jesus the son of Joseph of Nazareth. (Jn 1:45)
- Joseph also went up from Galilee out of the city of Nazareth into Judea, to the city of David which is called Bethlehem, because he was of the house and family of David, to be enrolled with Mary his espoused wife, who was with Child. And it came to pass that when they were there, her days were accomplished that she should be delivered. (Lk 2:4-6)
- They came with haste, and they found Mary and Joseph, and the Infant lying in the manger. (Luke 2:16)
- After the days of her purification according to the law of Moses were accomplished, they carried Him to Jerusalem, to present Him to the Lord. (Lk 2:22)
- When his parents brought in the Child Jesus, to do for Him according to the custom of the law, he [Simeon] also took Him into his arms, and said: Now Thou dost dismiss Thy servant, O Lord, according

to Thy word, in peace. And His father and mother were wondering at these things which were spoken concerning Him. (Lk 2:27-29, 33)

• After they had performed all things according to the law of the Lord, they returned into Galilee, into their city Nazareth. (Lk 2:39)

• After they were departed, behold an Angel of the Lord appeared in sleep to Joseph, saying: Arise and take the Child and His Mother, and fly into Egypt, and be there until I shall tell thee. For it will come to pass that Herod will seek the Child to destroy Him. Who arose, and took the Child, and His Mother by night, and retired into Egypt. (Mt 2:13-14)

• When Herod was dead, behold an Angel of the Lord appeared in sleep to Joseph in Egypt, saying: Arise, and take the Child and His Mother, and go into the land of Israel. For they are dead that sought the life of the Child. He arose, and took the Child and His Mother, and came into the land of Israel. But hearing that Archelaus reigned in Judea in the room of Herod his father, he was afraid to go thither: and being warned in sleep, retired into the quarters of Galilee. And coming, he dwelt in a city called Nazareth. (Mt 2:19-23)

• His parents went every year to Jerusalem at the solemn day of the Pasch. And when He was twelve years old, they going up to Jerusalem according to the custom of the feast, and having fulfilled the days, when they returned the Child Jesus remained in Jerusalem; and His parents knew it not. And thinking that He was in the company, they came a day's journey, and sought Him among their kinsfolk and acquaintance. And not finding Him, they returned into Jerusalem, seeking Him. (Lk 2:41-45.)

- And it came to pass that after three days they found Him in the Temple, sitting in the midst of the doctors, hearing them and asking them questions. And all that heard Him were astonished at His wisdom and His answers. And seeing Him, they wondered. And His Mother said to Him: Son, why hast Thou done so to us? Behold, Thy father and I have sought Thee sorrowing. (Lk 2:46, 48)

* * *

Appendix 2

The Holy Family Belonged to a Royal House

St. Joseph is often presented by progressivists simply as an everyday workman, and the Holy Family as a proletarian family. Nothing is further from the truth. St. Joseph was a Prince of royal blood and a Patriarch.

This commentary by St. Bernardine of Siena helps to focus the devotion of St. Joseph and the Holy Family in a true Catholic perspective:

"St. Joseph accomplished the mission of being the guardian and provider for Mary and Jesus most faithfully, and for this reason the Lord addressed him with those words: 'Well done, good and faithful servant, enter thou into the joy of thy Lord.' These words reveal in the great Saint a threefold state.

"The first describes in this holy man the state of nature, in which shines the nobility of his birth. The Lord said 'good servant' in reference to the noble nature that He conferred on him. In truth, he was from a patriarchal, royal and princely race. To better understand this, let us consider the natural nobility of the three members of the Family: Wife, Spouse and Child.

"The Blessed Virgin was nobler than any creature who had ever existed or ever will exist. St. Matthew, thrice listing the 14 generations from Abraham to Christ, shows that she descends from the 14 Patriarchs, 14 Kings and 14 Princes. St. Luke, also describing her nobility, goes back in his genealogy from Adam and Eve until the birth of Christ God.

"Christ, who has not mother in Heaven nor father on earth, received from the Virgin all His humanity, and consequently the ancestry that makes Him a son of David and gives Him brothers of noble origin. His Most Holy Mother gave Him this. The dignity of Prince, King and Patriarch of the whole Israeli people was established in view of the Most Holy Virgin, to clearly demonstrate that the corporal nobility given to the human genre in Adam was given by God principally to reach, through numerous generations, the Virgin Mary; and through her, to end in Christ, the Most Holy Son of God.

"St. Joseph was born of a patriarchal, royal and princely race in a direct line. St. Matthew establishes the direct line of all the fathers from Abraham to the spouse of the Virgin, clearly demonstrating that all patriarchal, royal and princely dignity came together in him.

"Instead of giving the genealogy of Mary, St. Matthew described that of St. Joseph, which seems to have only an accidental relation to that of Christ, for three reasons:

"*First*, to follow the custom of the Hebrews and of Holy Scriptures, which never establishes the genealogy through women or mothers, but always through men or fathers.

"*Second* and principally, because of the kinship, Mary and Joseph belonged to the same tribe, and were relatives.

"*Third*, he gave the genealogy of Joseph and not of Mary to show the excellence of their marriage, during which Christ was born, and wherein their union was so close that Joseph merited being called, and in a certain way he truly was, the father of Jesus Christ.

"Christ was, therefore, a Patriarch, King and Prince for He received from His Mother, from whom He received His substance, everything that other men receive from their mothers. For this reason, the Apostle says that He was born of Mary from the seed of David according to the flesh (Rom 1:3).

"St. Luke also describes the nobility of Christ ... This nobility was prophesized by the Patriarch Jacob when he said: 'The sons of thy father shall bow down to thee' (Gen 49:8), referring to the adoration of the Divinity. And he added: 'The scepter shall not be taken away from Judah' (Gen 49:10).

"Thus the Evangelists described the nobility of the Virgin and of Joseph to manifest the nobility of Christ. Joseph was, therefore, so noble that, so to speak, he gave temporal nobility to God in the person of Christ Jesus." [74]

* * *

---

74. St. Bernardine of Siena, *Saint Joseph* (São Paulo: Paulinas, 1956), pp. 17-23.

Appendix 3

CLARIFICATIONS

A passage in Sacred Scripture that relates to both St. Joseph and the Blessed Mother states: "Now there stood by the cross of Jesus His Mother, and His Mother's sister, Mary of Cleophas, and Mary Magdalen" (Jn 19:25). Because St. Anne was at an advanced age when she conceived the Blessed Mother, a unique supernatural event, the above passage has been a great source of confusion to many Catholics and is rarely explained from the pulpit. Pure logic would dictate that the mother of the Mother of God, Our Lord Jesus Christ, would certainly not have another daughter.

Confirming this logic, *The Catholic Encyclopedia*[75] furnishes the explanation as follows: "Alpheus according to Hegesippus (*Hist. eccl.* III, XI) was the brother of St. Joseph and was married to Mary of Cleophas. She would therefore be the sister-in-law of Holy Mary. This would not contradict the passage from John 19:25 because St. Jerome states clearly in his introduction to the *Latin Vulgate New Testament* that he does not distinguish between blood lines and in-laws.

---

75. Vol. IX, 1910 ed., p. 749.

In the Gospel of Luke 18:31-43, Jesus is referred to as the "Son of Man." This expression is often used in the New Testament. It seems reasonable to wonder why as the "Son of God," Jesus would refer to Himself as the "Son of Man." According to Fr. Vallejo in his discourse on St. Joseph and to *Butler's Lives of the Saints,* [76] Jesus referred to Himself often as the "Son of Man" because of His intense love for St. Joseph, His earthly foster-father, and because His Sacred Humanity proceeded from Mary Immaculate.

* * *

---

76. *Butler's Lives of the Saints*, Vol. I, "St. Joseph" (NY: P.J. Kenedy and Sons, 1956), p. 631